PLATO AND ARISTOTLE

An Introduction

GUY W. STROH
Rider College

Boyd & Fraser Publishing Company - San Francisco, California

Library of Congress Catalog Card Number: 75-117509

Published by Boyd & Fraser Publishing Company, San Francisco 94118

About the Author

Guy W. Stroh is Professor of Philosophy and Chairman of the Department at
Rider College. He received his A.B., M.A., and Ph.D. degrees from Princeton
University, where he held the Chancellor Green Fellowship (1953-1954) and
the Bamford Fellowship (1955-1956). Dr. Stroh is a member of the American
Philosophical Association. He is the author of *American Philosophy from
Edwards to Dewey, An Introduction,* published by D. Van Nostrand Company.

1 2 3 • 2 1 0

TABLE OF CONTENTS

PREFACE

This outline is intended to be used in connection with a one-semester introductory philosophy course that traces the development of Greek Philosophy from its sixth century B.C. origins through the two great systems of Plato and Aristotle. Such an outline and course of study presupposes the actual reading of selections from the philosophers themselves, i.e. the Dialogues of Plato and selections from the works of Aristotle.

The study of Greek Philosophy from its origins to Aristotle is well suited to introduce the student to philosophy as such for the following reasons:

(1) Since it starts at the very beginning of Western Philosophy, subsequent developments are dependent upon it.

(2) It presents a very clear, logical growth or development of philosophical issues.

(3) The Greeks, during the short period 600-322 B.C., formulated virtually all the main problems of philosophy and suggested many of the most important solutions to these problems.

(4) The period is sufficiently short to be treated in a one-semester college course.

The student is advised to note carefully the following two main points in his study of this outline:

(1) Any history of philosophy is not a collection of mere facts. It involves a logical development instead. That is, the important thing is not merely *what* a philosopher said but *why* he said it— what reasons are given for any position.

(2) Every philosophical position or solution is based upon some question or problem that the philosopher is trying to solve, and cannot be understood apart from these questions or problems.

This outline is designed to help the student in his study of philosophy by focusing attention on these two points—the logical development of issues and the presentation of philosophical solutions or anwers in connection with the problems upon which they are based.

INTRODUCTION

THE RELEVANCE OF PLATO AND ARISTOTLE

It was the ancient Greeks who gave us our idea of philosophy as a constant love and pursuit of wisdom. And it is Plato and Aristotle who offer us the richest and most penetrating sources of this wisdom. Almost all of what we know of Socrates and other earlier thinkers is based upon the great legacy of writings of Plato and Aristotle. Socrates wrote no philosophical works, but he has been immortalized in the dialogues of Plato. Pythagoras and other early thinkers have left no treatises of philosophy intact, but nevertheless, their ideas survive in the formulations that Plato and Aristotle provide for us. Virtually all the most important features of Greek life and culture—art, literature, politics, science—receive their most articulate and thoughtful formulations in the hands of Plato and Aristotle.

Consequently, the student who discovers Plato and Aristotle at the same time finds himself participating in their efforts to clarify and understand the most fundamental and far reaching questions about the nature of man, society, and man's place in the universe. Plato's idealism and Aristotle's naturalism are relevant to us today because they represent models of possibilities within our own thoughts. These philosophers have many things to teach us, not because they knew all the answers to all man's problems, but because they stated so clearly many of the basic questions.

Inspired by Socrates and other earlier thinkers, Plato was concerned with basic questions: What is really of value to us? How can anything be really known? How should man really live in order to be in harmony with himself and all other things? But he recognized that there is a fundamental difference between merely pretending to answer these questions and doing justice to them. He gave painstaking care in his dialogues to showing why hasty or simple answers to these questions are inadequate. This led him to one of the basic principles in his philosophy: the distinction between appearance and reality. If we want to know what is good or valuable, for example, we must be able to show why certain things only *seem* to be good while others really *are* good.

By looking at mere appearances we can never find anything that is really stable or truly good. The same principle applies to knowledge. Our senses, memory and opinions *seem* to give us knowledge. But we are often mistaken. Perception, memory or opinion without reason and understanding are unstable and superficial. Hence Plato finds that both knowledge and values imply the existence of stable, unchanging ideal forms or standards of judgment. True knowledge and genuine values must be free of the imperfections found in ever-changing appearances.

How then are we able to find and apprehend truths and values that are universal, stable and rational? Here Plato finds a clue in the study of mathematics. One proof that the mind has the innate power to overcome appearances lies in the fact that our knowledge of mathematics or geometry involves objects that are stable, universal and rational. Two plus two always was and always will be equal to four. Numbers are universals, as are geometrical objects and properties, covering all the cases of particular things (men, animals, trees etc.) falling under them. Numbers and geometrical objects are also rational. That is, we can prove truths about them by reason or thought alone. Mathematical objects are rational because they are ideals; they have no physical imperfections.

Plato's discovery of ideals is central to his whole philosophy and is especially important in his moral and political views. Morality and politics depend upon knowledge and education. For Plato this means that man must come to understand and live by the right ideals. Moral virtues are ideal goods discoverable by reason. Nothing that we can see with our eyes is really stable or absolutely right. Hence no existing man or no existing society will be able to serve as a perfect model of how we really should live. The only good society is an ideal state which our mind or reason can apprehend, but which can only be imperfectly realized in a physical sense. Thus there is always room for improvement in any particular existing society. For Plato, reason tells us that a really good and just society would be governed not by tyrants, mob rule or by warriors, but by wisdom: by those who really know what is best and who teach or demonstrate their wisdom. Wise rulers would be those who know how to distinguish between appearance and reality, and who have the desire to improve the society according to the ideal.

Although Plato's idealism is actively optimistic, it is not a philosophy that paints an ideal world beyond the clouds so that we can forget about the actual world in which we live. Plato's ideals are inherently functional. Because they are more stable and perfect than the natural world they outlive changing appearances or passing fancies. But because Plato calls for rational ideals he can accept no short cuts by way of mere opinion or compromise with careful reason. Plato expressed the idea that man has innate powers of rational understanding to apprehend what is true and good. Man's destiny, for Plato, is to strive to live a life of reason.

The idealism of reason in Plato has had an enormous influence on succeeding generations. But without doubt Plato's greatest influence was that which he had upon Aristotle, who was his greatest pupil. Aristotle shared Plato's belief in a life of reason.

Aristotle had a remarkable ability to absorb other thinkers' ideas, including those of Plato. Aristotle's works abound in references to and analyses of the ideas of his predecessors. Equally important is the fact that Aristotle was inherently a very creative and systematic thinker and equally as original as Plato. If Plato gave clear, classic expression to idealism as a philosophy and life of reason, it is Aristotle who gave equally clear and classic expression to naturalism as a philosophy and life of reason.

Plato placed logic and reason outside changing natural things. Aristotle, on the other hand, made careful studies of plants and animals, the heavens and the earth, and through these studies came to the conclusion that logic and reason lie in and not outside natural phenomena. The growth of an acorn into an oak or the development of an egg into a chicken, as well as the revolutions of the heavens, illustrated to Aristotle that nature itself is logical and rational if we study it in careful detail and if we employ the proper logical methods of research. Consequently, Aristotle is in effect the originator of our present idea of natural science with all its important subdivisions.

Every natural substance, for Aristotle, is a union of its matter and its form, which are distinguishable but inseparable in nature. But since matter means *potentiality* for Aristotle, and form *actuality*, every natural substance is subject to change, motion or alteration. The acorn has the matter or potentiality to become an oak, fire has the matter or potentiality to move upward, the eye has the matter or potentiality to see and so on. Changes in nature are not haphazard, irrational or purposeless; rather, they are regular, rational and purposeful. Everything in nature, according to Aristotle, is subject to what he terms its four explaining reasons or causes: a material cause, a formal cause, a moving cause and a final cause. These causes are necessary or logically essential conditions of anything coming to be, and it is the purpose of the natural sciences to find and study them. Of course, Aristotle admits the existence of accidental or chance occurrences. Not every acorn develops into an oak, not every eye is able to see. But these deviations are by their very nature exceptions not rules, and hence do not prove that nature is basically or generally not rational and orderly.

Aristotle is also the originator of logic as a discipline which furnishes the methods of proof for all scientific work. He does not agree with Plato that mathematics is the model for all the other sciences. Mathematics for Aristotle is only one of the three basic theoretical sciences. It must be distinguished from physics and metaphysics. Mathematics studies forms or formulas as separated from physical bodies as well as from the ultimate or first principles of all things. Hence mathematics is neither a physical science nor a study beyond physical things (metaphysical science). Mathematics in fact makes use of certain basic ideas which it is the business of logic and metaphysics (the science of first principles) to explain. For example, mathematics must make use of the primary axiom or law of thought called the principle of contradiction. This principle states that a statement cannot be true and not true at the same time. This principle is used by mathematics and by all the natural sciences as well, but it cannot be proven or justified by them since it is too basic; we would in fact have to use it or assume it in trying to demonstrate it.

Aristotle believed it necessary to study the proper methods, nature and limits of proof itself. The mastery of logical techniques for finding, proving and organizing truths is a necessary requisite for science and a life of reason. Aristotle's logical studies, including his famous theory of the syllogism, constitute some of his most important and enduring contributions to philosophy. His discovery of the syllogism is perhaps the greatest single achievement in the history of logic, for the syllogism isolates and identifies a clear model of deductive reasoning.

Aristotle's ethics and political philosophy follow the pattern of naturalism established in his physics and metaphysics. He agrees with Plato that moral virtue as well as the good society must be based on a life of reason. But Aristotle insists that reason is intrinsic not extrinsic to life, morality and society. Men are not born good or bad, but they become so depending upon training and habit. Man by nature has the power to develop moral and intellectual virtues, but the way he is brought up and the society in which he lives make all the difference. Moral and political behavior for Aristotle depend upon choices and decisions which can be guided by reason but which cannot be finally or absolutely fixed for all time. Ethics and politics consequently are practical and not theoretical sciences; they are concerned with knowledge not for its own sake but for the sake of action, and they involve variable rather than fixed or changeless circumstances. Just as the physical sciences must depend upon observation and experience for their facts so ethics and politics must also be based upon experience. Moral and political wisdom therefore do not arise simply from contemplating abstract ideals. Rather, they arise in men who can apply reason and logic to their experiences in life.

Naturalism in ethics and politics implies that moral and political decisions resemble those in the science of medicine more than those in the science of mathematics. To cure or improve the patient the doctor must use his observation of the facts and his experience as well as his power of reason. In a similar way, to know how to be courageous or just is analogous to knowing how to give not too much nor too little of a medicine to a particular patient. In ethics or in politics, as in nature, every individual is a union of form and matter, of universal and particular. Consequently, a life of reason is a life of discerning the reasoned fact, never the fact alone nor the reason alone. Aristotle's greatest relevance stems from the painstaking care with which he sought to keep reasons and facts together. Reasons without facts would be empty. Facts without reasons would be blind and chaotic. Hence the call for balance in a life of reason is essential to Aristotle's whole philosophy. It is also one of the main reasons why his naturalism has been so influential and why it is still relevant to our life and times.

PART ONE

FORERUNNERS of PLATO and ARISTOTLE

I. The Milesians: Thales, Anaximander and Anaximenes

(A) Materialism and Monism:

The Milesians, from Miletus in Asia Minor, about 600 B.C., began rational investigations of nature and became the first real philosophers (cosmologists) by uniting empirical research (particular observations of natural phenomena) and speculative reasoning (general explanations as to the causes of these phenomena). They went beyond mythical accounts of the cosmos and sought a single, material substance to explain all things.

(B) Basic Problem: *Substance.* What is the basic material or substance that supports the universe?

(C) Speculations:

(1) Thales: 585 B.C. (Water)

(a) Thales said that water is the one basic material substance. It changes into ice, mist, etc. and nourishes the whole universe.

(b) With this crude account Thales started philosophy in the direction of naturalistic explanation and opened the way for other thinkers to criticize his views and improve on them.

(2) Anaximander: 570 B.C. (Boundless Mass)

(a) Anaximander tried to improve on Thales by taking a more inclusive substance: Undifferentiated, boundless mass.

(b) He observed that water was too limited to support the whole universe and that water destroys fire; only a more inclusive, undifferentiated substance can make allowance for the existence of opposites in nature: moist and dry, hot and cold, etc.

(c) Therefore, Anaximander reasoned that the substance of all things is "boundless mass" from which specific things —earth, air, fire, water, etc.—are separated.

(3) Anaximenes: 550 B.C. (Air)

   (a) Anaximenes tried to improve on both Thales and Anaximander by agreeing with Anaximander that water is exhaustible and that the substance of the world must be boundless.

   (b) But Anaximenes also agreed with Thales that substance must be definite; it must be a particular natural substance.

   (c) Air, he reasoned, is both boundless and definite, a particular natural substance.

   (d) Air nourishes life; the soul breathes in air to live. By rarefaction (loosening) and condensation (packing) air becomes warm, cold, fire, liquid, and solid—in fact all things.

II. Pythagoras and the Pythagoreans

(A) Dualism and Number:

The Pythagoreans, from southern Italy, were a secret religious school (founded about 530 B.C. by Pythagoras). They pursued mathematical and philosophic studies as part of their way of life. Whereas the Milesians were materialists and monists, the Pythagoreans were idealists and dualists, finding ideal forms (numbers) and opposites (pairs) behind all things.

(B) Basic Problem: *Form*. What is the basic structure, form or pattern behind all things, even material things?

(C) Speculations:

   (1) Things are made from numbers. All is numerical. The heavens, earth, water, etc., all have measure. There is no matter without number.

   (2) Musical sounds depend on number; the length of string determines the pitch of notes; bodily health depends on right ratios of food.

   (3) The whole cosmos is geometrical, made of points which are based on the unit from which lines (2 points), planes (3 points), and solids (4 points) are derived.

   (4) The number 10 is the perfect number. It comprehends the

whole cosmos of points, lines, planes, and solids since 1 + 2 + 3 + 4 = 10.

(5) Numbers are supersensible and perfect. They have a divine and superior status, since they are orderly and everlasting.

(6) Numbers are dualistic, odd and even, representing the basic dualism in the universe between opposites, limited-unlimited, soul-body, good-evil, warm-cold, etc.

(7) The soul is immortal like the circle with no beginning or end. The body is mortal like the straight line with beginning and end.

III. Heraclitus: 500 B.C.

(A) Fire and Flux:

The Milesians assumed some permanent matter that changes into various forms and the Pythagoreans assumed some permanent forms (numbers) behind all changing matter. The next step, taken by Heraclitus, was to push this to the conclusion that everything changes. All is flux.

(B) Basic Problem: *Change.* If matter and form in the universe can both change, then how can there be any real permanence or permanent substance at all?

(C) Speculations:

(1) Heraclitus argued that change is absolute, self-sufficient; there is no need of any permanent substance at all.

(2) Water changes to air, air to fire, hot to cold, moist to dry. Nothing remains the same.

(3) Fire is taken as the symbol of incessant change in nature. Fire is not a substance but a process. Everything flows; the cosmos is like a river.

(4) Change is, however, orderly; it has a *logos* which reason can discern.

(5) Reason shows a unity in variety, a harmony in opposites, (the way up and the way down are one and the same).

(6) Permanence is an illusion of the senses, taking things superficially—not going deep enough into reason. When one thing is added another is taken away. What looks the same really changes.

IV. The Eleatics: **Parmenides and Zeno**

(A) Being and Permanence:

The Eleatic Philosophers, from Elea in southern Italy, reacted to what they considered contradictions in earlier thought and tried to develop a rigidly consistent philosophy of Being or Existence (Ontology). Parmenides presented the positive side or theory of permanent Being. Zeno presented the negative side or refutation of motion and plurality.

(B) Basic Problem: *Permanence.* How can absolute change or becoming exist or be thought, how can a thing be and not be? How can a unity have variety, how can there be a one and a many?

(C) Speculations:

(1) Parmenides: 495 B.C.

(a) That which is impossible to thought is impossible in Being or Reality.

(b) That which is, is; that which is not, is not. Being is; non-Being is not.

(c) Change or becoming is not real or full being; to become is not actually to be. Therefore, change or becoming is non-Being, non-existent.

(d) Being cannot change. Being cannot come from Being or non-Being, since it already is Being and something cannot come from nothing.

(e) Being is at rest, permanent, homogeneous, full, present, and one.

(f) Becoming, motion, change, difference, emptiness, the past, the future cannot be rationally thought because they do not really exist. They are illusions of the senses.

(g) Reason sees things really, as fixed, identical, present, full and unified.

(2) Zeno: 450 B.C.

    (a) Defended Eleatic position indirectly by reducing ideas of space, multiplicity and motion to absurdity (paradoxes).

    (b) If we assume that space exists, then it must exit in something, in some further space, and that space in some further space and so on to infinity which is impossible to be or to be thought.

    (c) If there are many things (plurality) then between any two there will be a third (their relation to one another) and between the third and one of the others a fourth and so on to infinity which is impossible.

    (d) (Race Course Paradox). It is impossible to traverse a race course, since in order to cover the whole, one must first cover half of the course and before that one must cover half of that and so on to infinity, which is impossible.

    (e) (Achilles Paradox). It is impossible for the swifter runner to catch the slower runner (tortoise) who has a head start, since by the time Achilles has made up the original lead, the tortoise has moved ahead a certain distance, and by the time Achilles makes up that new distance the tortoise has had a chance to move ahead a further distance and so on to infinity.

    (f) (The Arrow). The arrow in flight moves neither in the space in which it is, nor in the space in which it is not. The arrow in flight is really at rest, since in order to move over a distance AB the arrow must occupy all the spaces along AB equal to its own length. But when it occupies any space equal to its own length it is not moving. Therefore, the arrow in occupying all the spaces equal to its own length has not in reality moved at all.

    (g) Significance of Zeno's Paradoxes:

      By defending the Eleatic position in the form of paradoxes (intending to show the absurdity of the concepts of motion, plurality and space), Zeno became the originator of dialectical thought, that is, conceptual argumentation in terms of proof and refutation. His paradoxes clearly raise logical, not factual, questions—questions concerning the essential nature of the concepts of motion, space, etc. and their consistency. Such questions can only be resolved by logical analysis, and logical analysis was what Zeno was attempting.

V. Empedocles: 455 B.C.

(A) Four Elements:

Heraclitus made change absolute and the Eleatics made permanence absolute. Empedocles tried to work out a solution to this impasse—a reconcilation between change and permanence.

(B) Basic Problem: *Reconciliation*. How can both permanence and change co-exist?

(C) Speculations:

(1) Absolute change or becoming is impossible. The basis or elements of things can neither be created nor destroyed.

(2) Earth, air, fire and water are the four elements or roots of the universe.

(3) Everything is made from these four qualitatively different elements by combination and separation.

(4) The force of love brings the elements together; the force of hate tears them apart. The cosmos consists of recurring cycles of building and tearing down of combinations of the four elements.

(5) Knowledge and perception are based on like knowing like. Because we are made of fire we know or perceive fire, etc.

VI. Anaxagoras: 460 B.C.

(A) Unlimited Seeds:

Anaxagoras, like Empedocles, tried to find a compromise solution to the problem of change and tried to improve on Empedocles' conceptions of matter and the forces that cause it to change.

(B) Speculations:

(1) Anaxagoras agreed basically with Empedocles that creation and destruction do not really occur and that the universe is a plurality of basic elements mixing and unmixing.

(2) However, an unlimited number of seeds or portions is required to stock the entire universe, not just earth, air, fire and water.

(3) Mind or *Nous* is distinguished from matter: it is simple, unmixed; matter is essentially composite.

(4) In matter there is a portion of every other matter: in food there is bone, flesh, hair, etc; in the heavens there are earthly substances. The sun is a red hot stone.

(5) *Nous* or mind steers all things by orderly reason, not love and hate. The universe has purpose (teleology) by virtue of mental design.

(6) Perception is by opposites or contrasts, not by similars. Warm skin perceives the cold; cold skin the warm, etc.

VII. Democritus: 420 B.C.

(A) Atomism:

The Atomic Theory of Democritus is the final stage of early Greek Cosmology. The atomists tried to develop a comprehensive materialism and to simplify the solutions to the problems of substance, change and perception. Democritus also developed a theory of man and ethics and thereby set the stage for the next period of Greek thought—the period of humanism including the Sophists and Socrates.

(B) Problems: *Unity and diversity.* How can a total view of the universe be devised that will be comprehensive and consistent; how can substance and form, one and the many, perception and reason, mind and matter, man and nature all be united under one explanation?

(C) Speculations:

(1) There is only one kind of substance or matter: atoms, space-filling bodies which are qualitatively all the same, but quantitatively different. They differ in size and shape.

(2) There are an infinite number of these invisible, indivisible, dense bodies. They are one in substance but many in form— "sizes and shapes."

(3) There is only one kind of change—change of positions of the atoms. Atoms cannot be divided, destroyed or created physically, but they move by bombarding one another. Motion is inherent in the atoms.

(4) The void or empty space exists in order that the atoms may have a place in which to move.

(5) Everything is atomic—even the soul or mind. It is made of round, smooth atoms, and when its atoms disperse, death occurs.

(6) There is no purpose (teleology) in the atoms or in the universe, only necessity. Everything happens according to fixed motions of the atoms; nothing occurs at random.

(7) Perception is relative to changes in atoms passing through a medium and striking the senses. All sense qualities (colors, sounds) depend on quantities of atoms from a stimulus through a medium to the sense organs. Perception is subjective, conventional. The atoms have no colors, sounds. Perception indicates the effect that atoms have on our bodies.

(8) Only thought or reason, not the senses, knows the atoms, for they are too small to be observed.

(9) Thought or reason is superior to sensation, and the true guide for man's well-being.

(10) The good life for man is found in uprightness of character and fullness of understanding.

VIII. Sophists: 440-400 B.C.

(A) Humanism:

The Atomists helped prepare the way for an age concerned with man and subjective experience rather than nature and the objective world. The Atomists had made perception relative, conventional and subjective, emphasizing the importance of the subject in perception. The Sophists rejected cosmology and occupied themselves with the learning and teaching (for hire) of those subjects and methods needed in order to make man's life successful. The Sophists concerned themselves with politics, oratory, debate, morals, religion, and all forms of education that lead to making a success of oneself in the business of life. Objective truth gave way to subjective, knowledge gave way to opinion, and the search into reality gave way to looking for appearances. The art of persuasive reasoning (eristic) was cultivated, and winning an argument became more important than validating or proving an argument.

(1) Protagoras: (Man is the Measure)

(a) Protagoras epitomized the Sophistic position by holding that man is the measure of all things. According to Plato he considered knowledge to be based on subjective belief or opinion. What is true to me, is true. There is no objective criterion of truth or knowledge, only a subjective one from man's point of view.

    (b) However, one can learn the art of persuading someone to a position: one can learn to speak and argue to convince others and be successful.

    (c) As to the existence of the gods, Protagoras was an agnostic. Man cannot really know whether they exist or not.

(2) Gorgias: (Nihilism)

    (a) Gorgias developed an extreme form of subjectivism or skepticism, denying objective reality, knowledge and language.

    (b) He argued that nothing really exists; there is nothing to know.

    (c) Even if something existed we could not know it, since we can only experience ideas of things, not things themselves.

    (d) Even if we could get outside the prison of our own ideas and know things themselves, we could not communicate this knowledge because language or words are not the same as things. We would be communicating merely words, not knowledge.

IX. Socrates: 469 B.C.—399 B.C.

(A) Socratic Method:

Socrates saw more clearly than the Sophists the importance of man (the subject) in the questions of knowledge and conduct. The whole point of the Socratic philosophy is relentless, honest and consistent questioning, never assuming more than one can really prove. To live the good life one must question oneself and others as to what human excellence really is. In order to do this, one must search for clear meanings (definitions of virtues) and then justify these. This involves the cultivation of *self-knowledge* by *concepts* since without self-knowledge one is a victim of self-deception and without concepts one cannot find what is common and essential to many particulars.

(1) All knowledge is by way of concepts—universal definitions that cover all examples.

(2) All virtue or human excellence is by way of self-knowledge, since all virtue is a function of man's character or ability to master himself, which means knowing how to be temperate, just, honorable, etc.

(3) The greatest good for man is becoming wise concerning the improvement of one's soul (mind and character).

(4) The greatest harm is becoming foolish and corrupting one's moral qualities, i.e., one's integrity, justice, temperance, etc.

(5) All virtue is voluntary (responsible), based on knowledge; all vice is involuntary (irresponsible), based on lack of moral knowledge.

(6) By asserting the identity of knowledge and virtue, Socrates maintained the unity of man's thought (logic) and character (ethics) since, for Socrates, both depend on integrity, self-honesty or consistency.

(7) The Socratic philosophy, with its emphasis on logical method and moral goals or ends, is the proper bridge to Plato who developed under the strong influence of the Socratic method.

PART TWO

THE PHILOSOPHY of PLATO: 427-347 B.C.

I. Idealism

Plato's philosophy is the first great systematic statement of Idealism (asserting the identity of the real with the ideal). In its comprehensiveness it takes in all the main problems of previous thought and develops theories and doctrines to account for the entire scope of things, i.e., the cosmos and man's proper place in the cosmos. While its formulation is literary (Dialogues) its motive is moral and religious—to find a divine and perfect dimension for human existence and the salvation of the soul of man.

II. Relation of Plato to Earlier Philosophy

(A) From the Pythagoreans, Plato gets his dualism of Reality and Appearance—that which really is, as opposed to that which only seems to be. The material world is only an imperfect copy of an ideal, perfect world that exists in a transcendent world of Ideal Archetypes or Forms. The Pythagorean stress on mathematics is taken by Plato as the proper method of study to lead the mind out of the concrete into the abstract, out of particulars to universals. Immortality and reincarnation of the soul are accepted along with the conception of philosophy as a way of life (reaching salvation) as well as a method of study.

(B) From Heraclitus, Plato applies the idea of flux or change to the whole physical world—the world of appearance.

(C) From Parmenides, Plato accepts the identity of Reality as Being or Permanence. The absolutely Real World is fixed, rational and absolutely perfect.

(D) From Zeno, Plato makes use of the method of dialectical thought, that is, conceptual argumentation by way of proof and refutation.

(E) From Anaxagoras, Plato incorporates the idea of purpose or teleology in the universe. Mind or *Nous* governs the universe and designs things for the best.

(F) From the Atomists, Plato accepts the relativity of sense perception and the invisible character of reality. But in place of invisible material atoms, Plato calls for invisible, immaterial forms or Archetypes.

(G) From the Sophists, Plato accepts the challenge to establish the objectivity of truth, knowledge and values. The methods of argumentation, teaching of virtues, etc., all must be mastered. Appearances must be studied to learn the distinction between what is absolutely true or good and what only seems so.

(H) From Socrates, Plato accepts the notions that knowledge is only by way of conceptual thinking and that human excellence must be based on such knowledge. Plato therefore begins where Socrates left off and develops an entire philosophy built upon the Socratic method and inspired by the Socratic ideal. In fact, Socrates becomes the chief spokesman for philosophy in the Platonic dialogues.

III. Chronology of Writings

(A) Early dialogues: (*Apology, Crito, Euthyphro, Charmides*, etc.) Exercises in the Socratic method of formulation of definitions of moral concepts—negative insofar as no final resolution of the problem is reached.

(B) Middle dialogues: (*Phaedo, Republic, Symposium, Phaedrus*, etc.) Formation of Plato's own theories concerning Reality, Knowledge, Immortality, Ethics, Politics.

(C) Late dialogues: (*Parmenides, Sophist, Timaeus, Laws*, etc.) Deeper analysis of previous problems. Plato subjects his own earlier theories (especially that of Forms) to critical questioning, and works out in great detail a cosmology and political philosophy.

IV. Plato's Problems

(A) To work out a satisfactory theory of knowledge.

(B) To develop a theory of reality that is consistent with the nature of knowledge—an ontological system which is epistemologically grounded.

(C) To develop a theory of Good or Value including a Political and Ethical Philosophy.

(D) To develop a theory of the soul and justification for its immortality.

(E) To develop a cosmology that is not open to the objections applicable to earlier theories.

V. Plato's Theory of Knowledge

(A) Criteria of knowledge must include exactitude, reality and justification.

    (1) Genuine knowledge must be absolute, fixed and infallibly apprehended.

    (2) Genuine knowledge must be an apprehension of perfectly real, not illusory objects.

    (3) Genuine knowledge must be completely justified—based on thorough reasoning.

(B) Why sense perception is not knowledge:

    (1) Senses are inaccurate witnesses, giving conflicting reports and always changing.

    (2) Perception is always relative, never absolute—what we see or hear is never absolute beauty or harmony as it is in itself, but only as it appears relative to us.

    (3) Perception only uncovers a diversity of particulars—it does not reveal any universal, or that which is common and essential to many particulars.

    (4) Seeing or hearing is not understanding—else we would have knowledge of a foreign language just by seeing it or hearing it.

    (5) Perceptual objects are neither perfectly real nor intelligible—they are appearances not real objects of knowledge. We cannot observe any perfectly straight line, etc., only an approximation.

    (6) Perceptual experiences lack objectivity and justification. We cannot perceive or observe the why of things—the reason behind them.

(C) Why factual information is not knowledge:

    (1) Facts are never certain or absolute—they are relative (to inaccurate perception).

    (2) Facts are appearances, not real objects of knowledge—they are always changing and they make up a mere plurality of objects. It is impossible and senseless to know them all.

(3) Facts themselves need explanation—no fact explains itself or the why of things.

(D) Why opinion and even true opinion are not knowledge:

(1) Mere opinions may be true or false and are fluctuating.

(2) Even true opinion is not genuine knowledge, since it only tells us *that* a thing is so, not *why* it is so. And true opinions may be true for the wrong reasons.

(E) The Stages of Cognition:

(1) Knowledge is best understood by considering the development of awareness from the lowest forms to the highest or ideal form as presented in the *Republic*.

(2) Imagining (fleeting images and feeling) is the lowest form of awareness: it is uncertain, unreal and unjustified.

(3) Belief or opinion is a higher form of awareness—the recognition of objects, persons, places—but it is not absolutely certain; these objects are changing and only partially real and opinions about them are never fully justified.

(4) Mathematical thought is higher than opinion since it is more exact, deals with fixed unchanging (abstract) forms, and makes use of reason to prove its conclusions. Mathematics is not the highest form of cognition since it makes use of diagrams (appearances), and makes use of assumptions or hypothetical reasoning in its proofs, and is not completely justified.

(5) Philosophical thought is the highest form of awareness since it is purely abstract and exact, and does not depend on the senses or appearance. It deals with perfect universals or Forms and only essential characteristics or fixed principles. It dispenses with assumptions or hypothetical reasoning altogether and offers complete justification or proof. Philosophical thought terminates in direct awareness or insight into the highest object of knowledge (The Good) and answers the final *why* question—what is the good of anything? Until the Idea of Good is reached knowledge is incomplete, since all Forms or Essences are part of the Good and we do not really know what knowledge itself is until we know what purpose it has or what good it is.

VI. Plato's Theory of Forms

(A) The cornerstone of Plato's whole philosophy is his Theory of Forms in which he attempts to solve three fundamental problems:

    (1) What are the proper objects of knowledge? (epistemological problem)

    (2) What is the nature of Reality or Absolute Existence? (ontological problem)

    (3) What are the proper standards or goals of excellence? (ethical or teleological problem)

(B) Characteristics of Forms:

    (1) Logical identity or unity: for each group of particular things there is *one* Form or Essence that defines their nature, e.g., behind the *many* beautiful things in the world there is a single Form of Beauty.

    (2) Permanence: Every Form is unchanging, e.g., particular beautiful things are subject to alteration, but the Form of Beauty or Absolute Beauty is fixed, unalterable.

    (3) Universality: Every Form is a complete generality or universal, e.g., the Form of Beauty is universal and covers all the particular things that have some Beauty in them.

    (4) Eternity: Every Form is an eternal object, that is, timeless, with no beginning and no end.

    (5) Independent Existence: Forms are independent of matter and mind—they are neither mental nor physical objects—but possess their own logically independent Absolute Being.

    (6) Abstraction: Every Form is abstract as opposed to concrete and open only to thought; that is, Forms are not apprehended by the senses, but by the mind.

    (7) Perfection: Every Form is an Ideal or perfect object—incorruptible, possessing absolute value.

    (8) Hierarchy: Plato's Forms make up a hierarchy of universals with the Form of the Good or Goodness at the top. Every Form has some Good in it and the Good itself is the highest object of knowledge.

(C) Kinds of Forms:

  (1) Classes of things: Man, Bed, etc.

  (2) Qualities: Straightness, Roundness, Whiteness, etc.

  (3) Quantities: Oneness, Twoness, etc.

  (4) Relations: Equality, Difference, etc.

  (5) Values: Justice, Beauty, Goodness, etc.

(D) Purpose of Plato's Forms:

  (1) They serve as the proper objects of knowledge—they are the fixed, universal conceptions that Socrates was trying to find.

  (2) They make up Absolute Reality—they are the substance or underlying principle of things that the Pre-Socratic philosophers were trying to discover.

  (3) They determine and set fixed, universal values and goals for man and society—they are the standards of excellence that Socrates was searching for.

VII. Plato's Dualism: Appearance and Reality

(A) Reality for Plato is perfectly rational or orderly, that is, purely *ideal*. Reality is unchanging.

(B) Reality for Plato is transcendent—it is that which transcends or is beyond the changing, concrete world of sense perception.

(C) The World of Appearance for Plato is imperfect—an imperfect copy of the Ideal World of Reality.

(D) The World of Appearance is not unreal, but only partially real, that is, to a degree rational or orderly but not absolutely orderly.

(E) The World of Appearance is between Absolute Reality and Absolute Unreality. The World of Appearance or Change is an incomplete or unfinished world of becoming—between the Forms (Being) and Chaos (Non-Being).

VIII. Plato's Theory of the Soul

(A) The Soul for Plato is the link in the dualism of Appearance and Reality, since the Soul moves between or makes contact with both worlds. The Soul is the invisible life-force, self-animated, that is aware of both sensible things (Appearances) and abstract ideas (Reality).

(B) Parts of the Soul:

(1) The human Soul is divided into three parts based on the possible conflict of motives within the same individual: reason or the rational part, passion or the spirited part, and desire or the appetitive part.

(2) The function of the rational part of the Soul is to guide the other parts of the Soul by virtue of its knowledge or understanding.

(3) The function of the spirited part of the Soul is to enforce or side with the decisions of the rational part.

(4) The function of the appetitive part of the Soul is to obey or follow the rational and spirited parts in the satisfaction of desires.

(C) Virtues in the individual Soul:

(1) Plato accepts the views of Socrates, that moral excellence or virtue is based on self-knowledge through concepts and that the specific virtues form a unified whole.

(2) Wisom is the virtue or excellence belonging to the rational part of the Soul and implies knowing what is Good for the whole (Soul).

(3) Courage is the virtue appropriate to the spirited part of the Soul and implies knowing what should be feared (e.g. dishonorable death) and what should not be feared (e.g. honorable death).

(4) Temperance is the virtue which governs the desires or appetitive part of the Soul and involves knowing the right measure or limit in the satisfaction of wants.

(5) Justice is the virtue in the Soul that results when each part of the Soul is performing its proper function; that is, a Soul is just in which reason makes wise decisions, in which the spirited element enforces these decisions with courage and in which the desires obey the two higher elements with temperance.

IX. Plato's Ethics

(A) Plato's Ethics or Moral Philosophy is a direct consequence of his views on Knowledge, Reality and the Soul; that is, the Platonic Ethics combines epistemology with ontology and psychology.

(B) Moral knowledge cannot be based on perception, fact or opinion, since none of these are universal, unchanging or absolute.

(C) Moral knowledge must be based on Ideal Forms, since only they are universal, unchanging and absolute.

(D) Justice, Courage, Temperance and all the moral excellences are Ideal Forms or Ideal Standards of conduct, not descriptions of fact or the way things seem to be.

(E) Moral Values for Plato concern what ought (ideally) to be, not what appears in fact to be.

(F) The Virtues or Moral Values make up a unity rooted in the Soul and the Form of the Good. Every Virtue is a form of *self-know-ledge*. and every Virtue has some Good in it.

(G) The Concept of Platonic Love:

Plato views the development of moral excellence in the individual as a function of a blind, inborn impulse (termed *eros* or love), which must be given a rational direction. Morality is a function of striving or aspiration. In the *Symposium* this striving or aspiration is formulated in terms of a "ladder" or hierarchy of loves.

(1) The individual develops love for particular beautiful bodies.

(2) He must understand and love the kinship of all physical beauty.

(3) He must see the beauty of the Soul as higher than the first two.

(4) He must comprehend and love the beauty in avocations and social institutions.

(5) He must comprehend and love science and see that intellectual beauty is higher than all the preceding.

(6) Finally, he must become a lover of wisdom (a philosopher), and love the Form of Beauty itself and the other Forms, in-

cluding the Form of the Good which is the highest object of *eros* or Platonic love.

X. Plato's Theory of Education

(A) Plato's Theory of Education is selective (based on merit and innate aptitudes), graduated (based on orderly stages of development), and moral (based on cultivating the character and mind of the individual). All education is for the Soul insofar as the Soul is to take charge of the body.

(B) The first phase of education consists in a training or conditioning process to develop the character of the individual in terms of the senses, imagination, emotions and attitudes. Children are trained in right behavior through the use of good examples, e.g., stories of heroes, music, poetry, dramatic recitation and physical training.

(C) The first phase of education imparts no real knowledge but involves the proper use of appearances and even myth.

(D) The second phase of education is intended to impart knowledge gradually by developing the individual's power of thought or reason.

(E) In its moral emphasis the first stage of education is intended to give the individual true beliefs in the areas of moral attitudes and conduct. The second stage is intended for those whose aptitudes will enable them to go beyond true beliefs and understand the reasons why they are true.

(F) Higher Education:

    (1) The first step in higher education is to introduce the student to abstract thinking by the use of arithmetic or the theory of numbers (not to be confused with the art of calculation). Here, the student is expected to learn how to prove arithmetical propositions.

    (2) The second step is plane geometry, which involves the application of numbers to two dimensional (ideal) figures.

    (3) The third step is solid geometry, which involves the application of numbers to three dimensional (ideal) figures.

    (4) Astronomy is studied next as the science of the principles of the motions of three dimensional (ideal) heavenly bodies.

(5) Harmonics is studied as the science of the principles of ideal harmonies, which are only imperfectly found in physical sound or experience.

(6) Arithmetic, geometry, astronomy and harmonics are studied as *a priori* sciences, that is, in terms of fixed principles not based on the senses or experience, but rather on purified, abstract thought.

(7) Finally, Dialectic is studied as a comprehensive view taken of all the other sciences. Dialectical thought is based on the Socratic method of relentless, consistent and honest conceptual questioning of an issue in order to see all sides of the issue and render an impartial judgment or evaluation concerning the Good of anything.

(8) Plato identifies dialectical thought with philosophical thought. Only dialectical thought takes in pure, abstract Forms, removes assumptions by thorough reasoning and pursues the highest object of knowledge (The Good) to find the real value or significance of anything.

(G) Innate Ideas and Recollection:

(1) Plato holds that genuine knowledge cannot literally be put into the Soul, but must rather be drawn out of the Soul.

(2) Knowledge requires understanding and reasoning and these powers can only be developed from within and only given direction from without.

(3) This means that knowledge is innate in the Soul and has to be recollected in the process of questioning and answering. The Soul has the power to think, but is imprisoned in and distracted by the body and sensuous appearances.

(4) To obtain understanding (to become educated in the full sense), the Soul must overcome changing appearances and by its own power discern the unchanging, universal Forms or Reality, the proper objects of knowledge.

(H) Views on Art:

(1) Plato views art as a form of imitation—but an imitation or copy of mere appearances.

(2) Art therefore does not reveal any knowledge but is a deliberate form of illusion or deception and must be censored or controlled if it is to have any value.

(3) A drawing of a bed, for example, is twice removed from real-ity—since it is a two dimensional copy of a three dimensional physical bed and the three dimensional physical bed is itself only an imperfect, changing copy of the abstract form or essence of all beds.

(4) Art therefore is accorded an inferior status; it deals with particulars and appeals to the lower aspects of awareness—imagination, emotions and perceptions.

(5) Art therefore is primarily of use in the education of the young. For those whose mental powers are not fully developed it may be used to present likenesses or apparitions of moral qualities and harmonies.

XI. Plato's Social and Political Philosophy

(A) Plato's conception of the Ideal Society or *Republic* is based on his theory of Forms, and his Theory of the Soul or human nature. The Ideal Society must be perfect, that is, absolutely just, orderly and rational. Such an Ideal could never exist in fact or in the realm of changing particulars. The Ideal Society is intended as a standard of perfection, as an incentive to be approximated in the world of fact. In the Ideal Society the parts of the State correspond to the parts of the Soul, and individuals of the State are assigned positions solely according to their merit.

(B) Parts of the Ideal State:

(1) Rulers, made up of philosophers whose function is to direct the State solely in terms of their superior wisdom.

(2) Guardians, made up of auxiliaries to the rulers and whose function is to implement the wisdom of the rulers and maintain order in the society.

(3) Workers, made up of craftsmen, merchants and farmers whose function is to produce and distribute necessary goods for the whole state.

(C) Virtues in the State:

(1) Wisdom is the virtue of the Ruling Class which corresponds to the rational part of the Soul.

(2) Courage is the virtue of the Guardian Class which corresponds to the spirited part of the Soul.

(3) Temperance is the virtue of the Working Class (but belongs in the other classes as well) and corresponds to the appetitive part of the Soul.

(4) Justice is defined in the state as each class performing its proper function. A State is just in which wisdom rules the whole, courage enforces the rule, and temperance obeys.

(5) Ideal Justice involves the perfect well-being or happiness of both the classes and the individuals in the State, that is, it is good, both in itself and in its results. Injustice produces faction, quarrels, disunity and dissatisfactions, whereas Justice is a source of strength, harmony of interests, mutual respect and health in the State and in the individual.

(D) Inferior Types of Government: Departures from the Ideal State:

(1) A timocracy is the first form of inferior government and is based on military rather than philosophic rule—honor instead of wisdom.

(2) An oligarchy in the form of a plutocracy in the second form of inferior government, worse than a timocracy, since it is ruled not by a trained (honorable) class, but by a privileged class in terms of money interests with no wisdom and justice.

(3) A democracy is the third form of inferior government, worse than an oligarchy, since rule is in the hands of all including the worst, and all desires are given indiscriminate satisfaction. Issues are decided by vote, not by reason.

(4) Despotism is the lowest form of government. Unprincipled in its rule, it is based on force alone and allows for unlimited injustice or wickedness to preserve the tyrant in power.

XII. Plato's Theory of Immortality

(A) In his theory of Immortality presented in the *Phaedo*, Plato attempts to unite the various aspects of his total philosophy and to define the purpose and value of human existence. Socrates had taught that what is really worthwhile is not merely living, but living well. Plato develops this point into the view that the purpose of man's life must be defined in terms of the highest aspect of his nature (the rational part of the Soul) and in terms of a certain quality of existence (perfection or divinity—the Ideal Forms) which only the rational part of the Soul can reach. He therefore goes on to argue that the rational part of the Soul, by virtue of its power or ability to apprehend the perfect and eternal Forms, shares with them a divine or everlasting existence.

(B) Arguments for Immortality:

(1) Everything has its corresponding evil that tends to destroy it—rust in iron, etc. The corresponding evil in the Soul is vice or wickedness, but this only makes the Soul worse; it does not destroy it.

(2) Only like can know like. The Soul is able to know eternal Forms. Therefore it must be like the Forms; that is, everlasting.

(3) The Soul is able to form a *priori* conceptions—ideas of perfect Circularity, Beauty, Justice, etc. But these conceptions cannot be derived from experiences in this world, since nothing in this world is perfect. Hence, the Soul must have remembered these conceptions from a previous and more perfect existence.

(4) Just as oddness in numbers can never become even and no odd number can become its opposite, so life can never become its opposite and no Soul (whose essence is to have life) can become its opposite or die.

XIII. Plato's Cosmology

(A) The goal of philosophy, according to Plato, is insight into the structure and nature of the whole universe or Cosmos. Plato's Cosmology, therefore, gives completeness to his own philosophy and is derived from his theories of knowledge, Forms and the Soul.

(B) Since Cosmology deals with the question of the origin of the structure of the visible world, genuine knowledge or absolute truth is impossible concerning it. Knowledge is only possible in relation to Reality (Forms) or Being, whereas the whole created universe is a world of appearances, a world of change or becoming.

(C) Therefore, Plato presents his cosmology in the form of a myth or likely story, claiming no more than approximate opinion for his account of the origins of the universe.

(D) According to this story presented in the *Timaeus*, an all-good, but not all-powerful Soul or Demiurge fashioned the universe out of pre-existing chaos (unformed matter) using the pre-existing forms as models of every created thing.

(E) The world was made as orderly and geometrical as possible, but not perfect, since the matter or receptacle out of which it was made was irrational and resists reason and order to some extent.

(F) The receptacle (crude matter) and the patterns (perfect forms) were joined by the Demiurge (all-good Soul) to form an imperfect changing copy of an ideal, unchanging world.

(G) The Form of the Good was the leading Idea in terms of which things were formed, giving purpose to creation. Everything was made as good as possible.

(H) A World Soul was placed in the midst of things so that the world body would have a soul to lead it, or give it life. Individual souls were also placed in all organic things to make the world as good and purposeful as possible.

XIV. Plato's Significance and Influence

(A) Plato's ideas have exercised a greater influence for the whole of subsequent Western Culture than those of any other single thinker with the possible exception of Aristotle.

(B) Points of Significance:

(1) Plato stands as the originator of philosophy in the sense that he was the first to give careful and extensive attention to the problem of defining the nature of philosophy itself.

(2) Plato's Dialogues, principally in the character of Socrates, offer what is perhaps the best and most vivid depiction of the operations of philosophic thought ever devised.

(3) The originality of Plato's ideas, plus the penetrating character of his thought, make his political philosophy, theory of knowledge, theory of education, theory of the soul, theory of ideas, and cosmology landmarks in the history of thought.

(C) Points of Influence:

(1) Aristotle's Philosophy is unintelligible apart from Plato and Plato's influence.

(2) Through his school of philosophy, the Academy, Plato maintained an influence on many of the greatest minds in Greece for many generations.

(3) Neo-Platonic, Stoic, Epicurean, and Hellenistic philosophy in general, up to 529 A.D., exhibit the strong influence of Plato's ideas, both in a positive and negative sense.

(4) Medieval philosophy and theology show the influence of Plato, especially in problems concerning immortality and Cosmology.

(5) Modern philosophy and culture, up to the present, exhibit the influence of Plato in the extensive revivals, borrowings, criticisms and analyses of his thoughts.

PART THREE

THE PHILOSOPHY of ARISTOTLE: 384-322 B.C.

I. **Naturalism**

Aristotle spent approximately twenty years as a student in Plato's Academy. Gradually, he developed in his own system of thought, which in many respects was critical and independent of the Platonic Philosophy. Specifically, Aristotle rejects Plato's Dualism and Idealism in favor of a more scientific and naturalistic conception of Reality. The natural or physical universe is taken by Aristotle to be completely real, and change or becoming is interpreted as a logical or orderly sequence, to be studied by the various sciences. Whereas Plato separated Form from Matter, Aristotle finds them always united in nature. Whereas Plato separated the universal from the particular, Aristotle finds them always united in natural or real individual substances. And finally, whereas Plato's conception of the soul and ethical and political values was idealistic, Aristotle's is naturalistic, based upon a scientific view of man's nature and purpose.

II. **Relation of Aristotle to Plato and Earlier Thought**

(A) Aristotle views the earlier philosophers as foreshadowing his own conceptions of things, especially his Four Causes or four explaining principles in nature.

(B) The Milesians (water, air, etc.) had a partial glimpse of Aristotle's Material Cause, or that from which as basic material a thing comes into being.

(C) The Pythagoreans had a partial idea (numbers) of Aristotle's Formal Cause or the formula of a thing's essence, which is a necessary, although not a sufficient condition of a thing coming into existence.

(D) Empedocles (forces of love and hate) had some idea of Aristotle's Moving Cause or that principle from which a change begins to take place.

(E) Anaxagoras, with his concept of *Nous* had some idea of Aristotle's Final Cause, the end or that for the sake of which a thing is.

(F) Socrates is credited by Aristotle for recognizing the need of universal definitions and the process of induction by which general ideas are built up from particular cases.

(G) Plato's cosmology may be viewed as an inadequate mythical formulation of Aristotle's Four Causes.

Plato (cosmology)	Aristotle (Four Causes)
(1) Receptacle	(1) Material Cause
(2) Patterns	(2) Formal Cause
(3) Demiurge	(3) Moving Cause
(4) Good	(4) Final Cause

Whereas Plato's cosmological ingredients are only mythical and make up a likely story concerning the world's structure, Aristotle's Four Causes are necessary conditions of all natural change. Whereas Plato's causal agents are transcendent and work from the outside, Aristotle's are immanent and operate within nature, and produce natural rather than supernatural development.

(H) Plato is heavily attacked by Aristotle for making universals exist apart from changing particulars, giving them separate existence. In fact, Aristotle is critical of Plato's Dualism and Theory of Forms in several respects:

(1) If Forms are essences, they cannot be outside of things; but must be in the things of which they are the essential nature.

(2) If Forms are static and unchanging, then they cannot be used at all to explain change or changing things.

(3) Forms are unnecessary duplications of things leading to an infinite regress; e.g., if the universal man stands apart from Socrates, an individual man, then there arises a third man which is the relation between the two, etc., on to infinity.

III. Aristotle's Writings

(A) Many of Aristotle's actual writings have not survived, especially his early dialogues written along the lines of Plato's. For the most part, the works of Aristotle that have survived are his scientific writings, detailed treatises on specialized subjects and general or philosophical elaborations or commentaries on the scientific works.

(B) Divisions among Aristotle's Works:

(1) Logical writings, including the analysis of terms, propositions,

syllogisms, scientific demonstrations and other forms of reasoning (including) fallacies.

(2) Natural science or writings on astronomy, meteorology, matter and motion (physics proper), biology and psychology.

(3) Metaphysics or writings on substance, being, categories, first principles of science and unmoved mover (Divine Being).

(4) Ethical and political writings on moral and intellectual virtue and the good for man in society.

(5) Poetics or writings on the nature of epic poetry and tragedy.

IV. Aristotle's Problems

(A) To work out a satisfactory system and classification of the various sciences required to explain all things.

(B) To develop a satisfactory logic or instrument of inference or reasoning to serve as the backbone of all scientific knowledge or proof.

(C) To develop a physics or science of nature, to explain the entire physical world from the heavenly bodies to living things, including man.

(D) To develop a First Philosophy or metaphysics to explain the basic nature of reality or substance, to explain the relation between the universal and the particular, the formal and the material, the actual and the potential, and to investigate the nature of a non-physical substance or divine being.

(E) To develop a satisfactory conception of practical science, including ethics and politics.

(F) To develop a satisfactory conception of productive science or art.

V. Aristotle's System of Philosophy

(A) Five Parts:

(1) Logic—theory of inference or reasoning.

(2) Physics—theory of natural world.

(3) Metaphysics—theory of reality.

(4) Ethics and Politics—theory of good life for man.

(5) Poetics—theory of art.

VI. Classification of the Sciences

(A) Theoretical Science has as its purpose to acquire knowledge for its own sake. Includes physics, mathematics, metaphysics.

(B) Practical Science has as its purpose to acquire knowledge for the sake of action. Includes ethics and politics.

(C) Productive Science is concerned with knowledge for the sake of making useful or beautiful things. Includes poetics.

(D) Why logic is not classified as a Science:

(1) Aristotle thought of logic as a necessary preliminary discipline required to do any scientific work at all.

(2) As the instrument of correct reasoning, logic is more fundamental than any science and serves as the backbone or organizing principle of scientific knowledge itself.

VII. Aristotle's Logic

(A) Aristotle's logical works fall into six principal parts:

(1) Categories—analysis of terms or predicables.

(2) *De Interpretatione*—analysis of propositions.

(3) Prior Analytics—theory of the syllogism.

(4) Posterior Analytics—theory of scientific demonstration and knowledge.

(5) Topics—analysis of probable reasonings.

(6) Sophistic Elenchi—a study of fallacies.

(B) The Logic of Terms:

(1) Terms serve as the subjects and predicates of propositions, but as such they are neither true nor false.

(2) The most fundamental terms are those that refer to primary substances, distinct individuals such as Socrates, Plato, etc.

Such terms are neither asserted of other things nor present in other things, but are primary in the sense that other terms are asserted of them.

(3) Terms that refer to classes of primary substances, such as man, horse, animal, etc., are called secondary substances since they depend upon primary substances.

(4) Other terms refer to qualities; e.g., white; quantities; e.g., two units length; relations; e.g., greater than; place, time, etc.

(5) Terms differ in quality and quantity. They may be affirmative or negative. They may be universal, particular or singular.

(6) A term is universal or distributed if it refers to a class as a whole; e.g., all horses.

(7) A term is particular if it refers only to some part of a class, e.g., some horses.

(8) A term is singular if it refers to only one individual; e.g., this horse.

(C) The Logic of Propositions:

(1) A proposition is a sentence that is either true or false—an assertion or denial of one term by another term; e.g., All men are blind, or No men are blind.

(2) Propositions may be universal, particular or singular. (So called indefinite propositions, e.g., Pleasure is good, cannot be true or false until they are made definite).

(3) There are two principal forms of universal propositions, (A) All A is B, and (E), No A is B; and two principal forms of particular propositions, (I) Some A is B, and (O) Some A is not B.

(4) These four forms (A, E, I, O) are the only forms that Aristotle considers in the principal part of his logic, the theory of the syllogism.

(5) Immediate or non-syllogistic inference:
Aristotle allows the direct deduction or inference of one proposition from another.

(a) From All A is B, Some A is B can be inferred.

(b) From No A is B. Some A is not B can be inferred.

(c) From All A is B, Some B is A can be inferred.

(d) From No A is B, No B is A can be inferred.

(e) From Some A is B, Some B is A can be inferred.

(f) Two important inferences are not allowed: From All A is B, All B is A cannot be inferred. From Some A is not B, Some B is not A cannot be inferred.

(g) Immediate inference allows deducing the particular from the universal, but not vice-versa.

(6) Contradictory propositions: All A is B and Some A is not B are contradictory; they cannot both be true nor both be false. The same holds for No A is B and Some A is B.

(7) Contrary propositions: All A is B and No A is B are contraries; they can both be false, but they cannot both be true. Some A is B and Some A is not B are subcontraries; they can both be true, but cannot both be false.

(D) Syllogism:

(1) A syllogism—All A is B, All B is C, therefore, All A is C—is a form of argument or reasoning, consisting of two propositions (the premisses) from which a third proposition (the conclusion) is asserted to follow by necessity.

(2) A syllogism must contain three categorical propositions of the A, E, I, O forms and exactly three terms, each of which is used in the same sense throughout the argument.

(3) Any syllogism is either valid or invalid depending upon whether or not the conclusion follows necessarily by deduction from its premisses.

(4) Rules sufficient to determine validity of any syllogism:

(Rule 1) The term common to both premisses (called middle term) must be universal or distributed in at least one premise.

(Rule 2) If a term is universal or distributed in the conclusion, that term must be universal or distributed in one premise.

(Rule 3) If one of the premisses is negative, the conclusion must be negative.

(Rule 4) From two negative premisses no conclusion follows.

(Rule 5) If the conclusion is negative, one of the premisses must be negative.

(5) Aristotle's Three Laws of Thought are three principles which are so basic to all logical discourse that any attempted proof of them would have to assume them.

(Law 1) Law of Identity (A is A)—any attribute is what it is and not anything else.

(Law 2) Law of Contradiction (not both A and not A)—the same attribute cannot at the same time belong and not belong to the same subject in the same respect.

(Law 3) Law of Excluded Middle (either A or not A)—either an attribute belongs or does not belong to some subject.

(E) Scientific Demonstration and Knowledge:

(1) A scientific demonstration is a syllogism whose premisses are basic truths of a certain science and whose conclusion is a necessary or proven truth of that science.

(2) The proper object of scientific knowledge is something which cannot be otherwise than it is.

(3) Scientific knowledge, therefore, is knowledge of the reasoned fact; we know scientifically when we know why a thing is the way it is and why it cannot be otherwise.

(4) Science requires induction (the method of inferring the universal from the particular) to discover its basic universal truths. Induction is, however, only a preliminary to scientific knowledge since these universal, induced truths must be used to demonstrate or deduce a particular (necessary) conclusion before genuine scientific knowledge is reached.

(5) Science requires definitions (statements of the essential characteristics, i.e. genus and differentia of its terms) in order to formulate the essential *whatness* of a thing.

(6) A science cannot demonstrate its basic truths. Scientific proof is not possible of the primary premisses of a science since all proofs must be finite and no proof can be circular.

(7) Scientific knowledge is not possible through the act of perception, since perception does not reveal the reasoned fact, but only the bare fact. Perception does not reveal the universal cause upon which the fact depends.

(8) Scientific knowledge differs from opinion in that scientific knowledge is the apprehension of the way a thing must be, whereas opinion is only the apprehension of the way a thing may be.

(9) There can be no scientific knowledge of accidental or chance happenings since they exist neither universally nor by necessity.

(F) Classifications of Fallacies: A fallacy is any line of reasoning or argument that only seems to prove or refute a point, but which in reality does not do so. Fallacies are divided into two basic kinds (verbal and non-verbal) with various illustrations of each.

 (1) Verbal Fallacies: Reasoning that goes astray because of confusions in the meanings of words.
   (a) Equivocation: A single word being used in several different senses throughout an argument.

   (b) Amphiboly: Ambiguity in sentence structure.

   (c) Composition: Putting words together incorrectly.

   (d) Division: Incorrect separation of words.

 (2) Non-Verbal Fallacies: Fallacies which do not depend on verbal confusions, but rather on logical irrelevance.

   (a) Accident: Taking what is true of a thing in its essential nature as true of each of its accidents.

   (b) False Refutation: Not realizing what refutation implies.

   (c) Circular Reasoning: Proving a proposition by assuming the very proposition to be proved.

   (d) False Conversion: Converting a proposition which cannot be converted; e.g., if some humans are not Greeks it is a fallacy to argue that therefore some Greeks are not humans.

   (e) Complex Question: Asking a question that improperly assumes answers to prior questions.

VIII. Aristotle's Physics

(A) Subject-matter: Physics is one of the theoretical sciences; its purpose is to acquire knowledge of nature for its own sake.

(B) Distinction between Physics and Mathematics: whereas mathematics studies forms or formulas in separation from matter, physics studies forms that are inseparable from matter. For example, mathematics and physics both are concerned with volume, but mathematics is concerned with the abstract formula of volume apart from any material thing. Physics studies volume as applied to some material thing or body.

(C) Distinction between Physics and Metaphysics: Physics limits its investigations to material substances or material being, whereas metaphysics studies substance in general, or being as such. Physics studies one kind of being, physical being, whereas meta-physics investigates the whole category or concept of being.

(D) Parts of Physics:

(1) Physics proper studies all matter that is movable, changeable.

(2) Astronomy is that part of physics which studies celestial matter, which only changes in one way according to Aristotle, that is, by moving in space.

(3) Meteorology is that part of physics which studies phenomena between celestial and terrestrial bodies; e.g., rainbows, clouds, etc.

(4) Geology is that part of physics that studies composition and changes of terrestrial matter, which Aristotle believed to be fundamentally earth, water, air and fire.

(5) Biology is that part of physics which investigates organic matter, matter that has "soul" in it; e.g., plants and animals.

(6) Psychology is that part of physics which investigates the essential life functions or soul of living things.

(E) Key Concepts of Physics:

(1) Matter and Form: All physical phenomena have both matter and form which are inseparable but relative. Matter is the crude stuff of which the form is the shape or structure; e.g.,

bronze would be the matter of a bronze statue, and the human shape may be the form or structure of the statue.

(2) Potentiality and Actuality: Matter is always capable of change; form is always a determinate structure or realization. Hence, matter is a potentiality of a thing to change and form some actuality or definite realization.

(3) Motion and Change: Matter and Form, Potentiality, and Actuality imply change since change requires some matter to be changed and some form to be changed to; e.g., an acorn is the matter relative to an oak which is the realized form, and the acorn has the potentiality to become an oak, and the oak is the actuality or realization of the acorn.

(4) Four Causes: The Four Causes or necessary conditions of change are required to explain any material change.

    (a) Material Cause: That from which as necessary material a thing comes into being; e.g., a wood fire cannot come into being without the wood.

    (b) Formal Cause: The form or structure a thing must have in order to come into being; e.g., a wood fire cannot come into being without the combustibility of the wood. The wood must be in a certain form to burn.

    (c) Moving Cause: That principle which moves or unites the form with the matter; e.g., a wood fire cannot come into being without something to ignite the combustible wood.

    (d) Final Cause: The end or that for the sake of which the thing is; e.g., the wood fire is that end or that for the sake of which the other causes exist—the wood, its combustibility, its being ignited.

(5) Distinction between Essence and Accident: The essential characteristics of a thing are those without which the thing cannot exist; the accidental characteristics are incidental or those which a thing may have, but does not have to have. For example, if man is by definition a rational animal, then being rational is essential, but having red hair is not essential, but accidental.

(6) Makeup of Physical Universe:

    (a) The earth is motionless and located at the center of the universe.

(b) The physical universe is finite and extends to the outermost ring of the stars.

(c) There are five basic kinds of matter in the universe, each with its natural place. Earth, the heaviest matter; water next and lighter than earth; air next and lighter than water; fire next and lighter than air; and aether, or fifth element, imperishable and located in all celestial bodies.

(d) The heavenly bodies move in circular paths around the earth, and their movement implies continuous or eternal motion to counter-balance the eternal rest or immobility of the earth.

IX. The Life Sciences: Biology and Psychology

(A) Biology and Psychology are both parts of physics, since both must study the material as well as the formal conditions or aspects of life and living things.

(B) Scale of living things: All living or organic things possess the power of self-maintenance, nutrition and growth. Plants are the simplest living things and lack sensation and locomotion which is characteristic of all animals. Men possess reason, which animals lack, and thus are the highest forms of living things.

(C) Natural Teleology: All living things possess an innate impulse to develop or grow in a definite direction; e.g., the acorn develops into the oak, etc.; and the parts of living things have a definite function in relation to the maintenance of life in that organism; e.g., heart for pumping blood, teeth for chewing food, etc.

(D) Psychology is concerned with the essential nature of the soul or life principle itself.

(E) The soul or principle of life is defined as the first grade of actuality of a natural, organized body having life potentially in it. First grade of actuality implies a power or function capable of being exercised, but not necessarily being exercised.

(F) Relation of Soul to Body: The soul is related to the body as form is related to matter. The soul is the form a body takes when it has life; the body is the instrument of life, e.g., if an eye were an animal, sight would be its soul, since sight is the proper function of the eye.

(G) The soul cannot be a body nor be without a body, e.g., sight is not the eye nor can it exist without the eye.

(H) The soul includes all life functions, and psychology is the study of their nature; i.e., perception, memory, touch, reasoning, etc.

(I) Perception is distinguished from reason in that perception receives the sensible forms of things; e.g., colors, sounds of water, etc. and reason receives the intelligible or essential forms of things, e.g., the essence of water formulated by its basic definition.

X. Metaphysics or First Philosophy

(A) Whereas the function of physics and the special sciences is to acquire knowledge, it is the function of metaphysics or First Philosophy to acquire widsom, that is, an understanding of the whole (being), not merely an understanding of the parts (celestial beings, terrestrial beings, etc.). Metaphysics inquires into the first or basic principles of all things.

(B) Metaphysics inquires into being *qua* being, which signifies substance in the primary sense.

(C) Substance means independent being, or full being—those entities which are fundamental and not dependent on or derived from anything else.

(D) Aristotle lists three kinds of primary substances:

(1) Terrestrial: perishable, sensible; e.g., Socrates.

(2) Celestial: imperishable, sensible; e.g., the sun.

(3) Divine: non-perishable, unmovable; e.g., God, Unmoved Mover.

(E) Primary substances make up reality for Aristotle since the real in nature comprises individual things, plants, animals, etc. The real outside of nature, or divine reality, also implies individual or entitative being, God or the Unmoved Mover.

(F) Universals are not substantial: qualities, quantities, and relations are derivatives of substances; for example, white has no existence apart from white things, two from two things, motion from moving things, etc.

(G) Aristotle's conception of reality is in sharp contrast to Plato's. For Plato, reality meant universals or essences outside or beyond particular things or exemplifications. For Aristotle, reality signifies universals or essences together with or in particular things or exemplifications. For example, Aristotle considers that Socrates, the individual man, is real insofar as he is both a particular being and a particular being of a certain sort, that is, with certain general or universal characteristics. Every real thing is both general and particular.

(H) Ontological Scheme: The Concepts of form, matter, actuality, potentiality, and Four Causes all have ontological significance; that is they are used by Aristotle to explain what in fact have existence or reality.

  (1) At the top of the ontological scale is Divine substance, pure form, pure actuality, that is, reality free from any change or matter.

  (2) Below pure form is form and matter together in nature where all things have potentiality and actuality, where things have a potentiality to change in a definite direction or line of development. The Four Causes are the principles used to explain this development in nature of things from matter to form; e.g., acorn—oak, etc.

  (3) Below nature or the unity of matter and form is pure matter which is only a negative concept since nothing exists that is pure matter without any form.

(I) Eternity of matter, form, motion: Neither matter, form nor motion comes into being, but only particular things made of matter and form can come into being or move. As basic concepts, matter, form and motion are reasons behind substances, explaining causes.

(J) No infinite series of causes: The explaining reasons for things cannot extend to infinity, else knowledge would be impossible; also there is no actual infinite.

(K) Solution of Zeno's Paradoxes: There is no actual infinite, either by way of division or addition, but rather the infinite is only a potentiality by way of addition or division. Numbers, for example, potentially can be added without end, but not actually. Space and time are only potentially divisible without end, not actually.

(L) Time, which is the measure of motion in terms of a before and after, cannot have a beginning or end, since motion, of which time is the measure, is eternal, and if time had a beginning or end we would still need time to determine its beginning or end.

(M) The Unmoved Mover—A final cause of all motion:

    (1) Motion is eternal, without beginning or end.

    (2) Motion involves potentiality and actuality—matter and form —something to be moved and something to do the moving.

    (3) There is no actual infinite.

    (4) From which it follows that there must be a final cause or reason behind all motion that is itself motionless.

    (5) The unmoved mover did not originate motion, since motion is eternal, but the unmoved mover is a logical not temporal starting point or premise from which motion is explained.

    (6) Motion or change in the universe involves a process in the direction of final causes or completion of development, of which the divine substance is the final cause, as that which is fully realized or actual.

    (7) The unmoved mover is pure actuality, pure mind, whose only function is contemplation. Aristotle's God is thought thinking thought.

XI. Practical Science, Ethics and Politics

(A) Purpose of Practical Science: To obtain knowledge for the sake of action, to obtain knowledge of what is the good for man in the moral sphere and in the political.

(B) Subject-Matter: Moral and political phenomena fall into the area of contingent things that depend upon choice and deliberation. That is, moral and political phenomena are not things which cannot be otherwise than they are, but rather they can be altered by human choice for good or for bad.

(C) Ethics is part of the subject matter of politics, since politics is concerned with the complete well-being of man in society, whereas Ethics is concerned with virtue or excellence of the soul.

(D) Practical Knowledge: Demonstrative or scientific knowledge is not possible in the practical sphere where phenomena are contingent rather than necessary, and where the particular case is more important than the general rule. Ethics and politics require choices and decisions that are relative to variable circumstances and cannot be absolutely fixed for each and every case.

ARAB WOMEN OF PHILADELPHIA

invite you to share the joys of
helping a child affected by war

ARABIC DINNER
ARABIC MOVIE

Sponsored by the

ORGANIZATION OF ARAB STUDENTS, PHILADELPHIA

Donation: $5.00 Adults   A   079

Received by _____

Time:4:30-9:30, Sunday, December 2, 1973

Place: 2nd floor, Houston Hall, Univ. of Penn.
        34th & Spruce Sts., Phila.

Buddism
Imperialism
Set name + book

German
Greek

look up Clb
Quint — ✓
History ✓

(E) The Good for Man: Happiness or rational well-being is the Good for man. This requires many ingredients: health, virtue, leisure, pleasure, proper development, etc. It involves the enjoyment of noble or good things for their own sake.

(F) The Good Life is a Life of Reason: Since man is by nature a rational animal, that is, a being with both reason and impulse or desire, the good life for man will depend upon the development of moral and intellectual virtues, virtues pertaining to the satisfactions of the desires and the reason.

(G) Moral and Intellectual Virtue: Virtue is cultivated by training and education; man is not born good or bad, but is made good or bad by practice or habit.

   (1) Chief intellectual virtues: science, art, practical wisdom, philosophic wisdom.

   (2) Chief moral virtues: courage, temperance, justice.

(H) Moral Virtue: Virtue is a state of character involving a choice of a relative mean. This mean, relative to man's nature, is determined by a rational principle and by that principle by which the man of practical wisdom would determine it. For example, courage is a mean between two extremes or vices: cowardice and rashness.

(I) In Opposition to Socrates: Moral virtue is not identical with knowledge, since if it were moral weakness and wickedness would be involuntary and not blameworthy. Moral virtue depends on both right reason and right desire. Moral virtue and wickedness are voluntary; both depend upon man's choosing on the one hand something praiseworthy and on the other hand something blameworthy.

(J) In Opposition to Plato: Moral virtues are not unchanging Ideals imperfectly copied by humans. Rather, moral virtues are in fact what the good man does and enjoys. In morals the proper standard is the good man and not the abstract good, since Ethics is concerned with the good for man that is attainable in practice, which means specific goods in relation to variable conditions and human nature.

XII. Political Philosophy

(A) The purpose of political philosophy is to acquire an understanding of the nature of man as a political animal in order that the best obtainable form of government may be achieved.

(B) Political philosophy depends upon political wisdom and is the practical science with the highest authority, since it decides questions affecting all matters of human life, including the place and proper function of the individual, the family, science, art, etc., in the larger whole or the state.

(C) Concept of the State: The State is the highest form of civic community (more complete than the family or village, etc.), since it aims at the most complete good for man.

(D) Priority or Fundamental Nature of the State: The State is the final cause of its individual members or parts. Only the State aims at the most complete good for man while its parts, individuals, aim at particular goods.

(E) Man is by nature a political animal: Man's proper development or end is rational and this can only occur in a larger rational whole. Man cannot attain happiness apart from the development of moral and intellectual virtues, and these can exist and flourish only under the protection and authority of some state.

(F) Citizenship: He who has the power to take part in the deliberative or judicial administration of any state is said to be a citizen of that state.

(G) Slavery: The Slave is a piece of property which is animate and fit for action rather than production.

    (1) Natural Slavery: Human beings who without being able to exercise reason for their own good or for others, but who at the same time are able to follow or obey the reason of others, are natural slaves.

    (2) The natural slave, according to Aristotle, benefits by subjection to a master.

    (3) Unnatural slavery, prisoners of war for example, is only conventional and is not based on reason or nature.

(H) Various Forms of Government: States may be classified in terms of the make-up (kinds) and the quality (goodness or badness) of their rule.

(I) Good Forms of Government: Those which have a regard for the common interest and in which their citizens truly participate in the advantages of the state, are good or in accord with justice.

(1) Royalty is rule by one for the common good.

(2) Aristocracy is rule by the few for the good of all.

(3) Constitutional Government is rule by the many for the common good.

(J) Bad Forms of Government: Those States which are based on satisfying the interests of a privileged class, and in which all the citizens do not truly participate in the State's advantages, are bad.

(1) Tyranny is a kind of monarchy which has in view the interest of the monarch only.

(2) Oligarchy has in view the interests of the wealthy and not the good of all.

(3) Democracy has in view the interests of the needy rather than the good of the whole.

(K) The Best Constitution for Most States: Aristotle, in sharp contrast to Plato, regards the concept of an absolute or ideally perfect state as irrelevant to the true purposes of political philosophy insofar as politics is concerned with practical, not theoretical knowledge.

(1) The best states are composed of citizens and cities which are equals as far as possible; these are generally the middle classes.

(2) The best political community is formed by citizens of the middle class, and those states are likely to be well-administered in which the middle class is large and stronger than the lower class (excessively poor) and the upper class (excessively rich).

(L) The best States are limited in size and number of citizens and follow a rational principle, as their citizens are guided by reason. This is most possible where the middle classes are dominant. They have neither too much nor too little by way of possessions. Those men who are neither in dire poverty nor excessive wealth are best able to make rational choices and decisions.

XIII. Aristotle's Theory of Art

(A) Art comes under the heading of productive science; that is, knowledge of how to make beautiful or useful objects. Its objects are contingent, not necessary, that is, they can be otherwise than they are; they can be modified by human desire and skill.

(B) As a form of knowledge, art involves the recognition of the universal as well as the individual included in the universal; e.g., housebuilding depends upon knowing certain elements pertaining to all houses or houses in general as well as those which apply only to some or even one individual house. Every artifact, like every substance, is both universal and particular, i.e., a particular object of a general kind.

(C) In Opposition to Plato: Fine art (poetry, sculpture, drama, etc.) is viewed by Aristotle as involving intellectual virtue and as a worthwhile pursuit of leisure. Aristotle agrees with Plato that art is a form of imitation or representation but rejects the view that it imitates particulars (appearances) rather than universals (reality). Art for Aristotle has intellectual content and philosophic significance precisely because it is able to imitate universal types. For example, in fine art noble characters or figures may be drawn that represent universal and morally significant types of action.

(D) Tragedy the Highest Form of Poetry: Tragedy is the dramatic imitation of an action of great magnitude which is serious and complete, and which purges the spectator of the emotions of pity and fear with the aid of such accessories as appropriate diction, thought, spectacle, and melody.

XIV. Significance and Influence of Aristotle's Philosophy

(A) In its breadth and detail Aristotle's philosophy remains, along with Plato's, one of the two most influential systems of thought ever devised.

(B) Points of Significance:

(1) Aristotle's Naturalism stands as a classic alternative to Plato's Idealism.

(2) Aristotle stands as the originator of logic, and as the proponent of the view that logic is the essence of philosophy itself.

(3) The wealth of Aristotle's scientific studies attests not only to his status as perhaps the greatest scientist of the ancient world, but also substantiates his own view that philosophy must be scientific and based on fact.

(4) The maturity and carefulness of Aristotle's humanistic studies (ethics, politics, etc.) indicate what is possible by way of a philosophy of man based upon reasoned facts rather than reason alone.

(C) Points of Influence:

(1) Aristotle virtually dwarfed all succeeding ancient philosophers in his learning and logical methods.

(2) Through his own school of philosophy, the Lyceum, he influenced succeeding generations of thinkers and successfully challenged Plato's authority.

(3) Medieval thought and philosophy were virtually dominated by Aristotle's methods, arguments and terminology.

(4) Modern science and thought could only come into its own by challenging Aristotle and by rethinking the problems and solutions he posed.

(5) The extensive borrowing from, revival, criticism, and analysis of his philosophy up to the present indicates the powerful influence that he has had and still has.

SUGGESTED READINGS

General Reference and Histories

BAKEWELL, CHARLES: *A Source Book in Ancient Philosophy*. New York, Scribner, 1939.

*CORNFORD, FRANCIS: *Before and After Socrates*. Cambridge, Eng., Cambridge U. Press, 1950.

*FARRINGTON, BENJAMIN: *Greek Science*. London, Penguin Books, 1953.

*GUTHRIE, WILLIAM: *The Greek Philosophers from Thales to Aristitle*. New York, Harper & Bros., 1960.

*RUNES, DAGOBERT: *A Dictionary of Philosophy*. New York, Philosophical Library, 1962.

*SAMBURSKY, SAMUEL: *The Physical World of the Greeks*. London, Routledge & Paul, 1956.

*SEYFFERT, OSKAR: *A Dictionary of Classical Antiquities*. New York, Meridan Books, 1956.

*STACE, W.T.: *A Critical History of Greek Philosophy*. London, Macmillan, 1967.

*WINDLEBAND, W.: *History of Ancient Philosophy*. New York, Dover Publications, 1956.

*ZELLER, EDUARD: *Outlines of the History of Greek Philosophy*. New York, Meridian Books, 1955.

Forerunners of Plato and Aristotle

*BURNET, JOHN: *Early Greek Philosophy*. New York, Meridian Books, 1957.

FREEMAN, KATHLEEN: *Companion to the Pre-Socratic Philosophers*. Cambridge, Mass., Harvard U. Press, 1957.

*KIRK and RAVEN: *The Pre-Socratic Philosophers*. New York, Cambridge U. Press, 1957.

*LEVIN, R.: *The Question of Socrates*. New York, Harcourt, Brace and World, 1961.

*Paperback Book

NAHM, MILTON: *Selections from Early Greek Philosophy.* New York, Appleton-Century-Crofts, 3rd Edition, 1947.

*TAYLOR, A.E.: *Socrates, The Man and His Thought.* New York, Doubleday Anchor Books, 1952.

Plato

*CORNFORD, FRANCIS: *Plato's Cosmology.* New York, Liberal Arts Press, 1957.

*CORNFORD, FRANCIS: *Plato's Theory of Knowledge.* New York, Liberal Arts Press, 1957.

*CORNFORD, FRANCIS: *The Republic of Plato.* New York, Oxford U. Press, 1958.

FIELD, G.C.: *The Philosophy of Plato.* London, Oxford U. Press, 1961.

FRIEDLANDER, P.: *Plato, An Introduction.* New York, Pantheon Books, 1958.

JOWETT, B. (trans.): *The Dialogues of Plato.* New York, Random House, 1937.

NETTLESHIP, R.L.: *Lectures on the Republic of Plato.* London, Macmillan & Co., 1937.

ROSS, DAVID: *Plato's Theory of Ideas.* London, Oxford U. Press, 1953.

*TAYLOR, A.E.: *Plato, The Man and His Work.* London, Methuen & Co. 6th Edition, 1949.

*TAYLOR, A.E.: *The Mind of Plato.* Michigan, Ann Arbor Books, 1960.

Aristotle

ALLAN, B.J.: *The Philosophy of Aristotle.* New York & London, Oxford U. Press, 1952.

*BAMBROUGH, R.: *The Philosophy of Aristotle.* New York, Mentor Books, 1963.

GRENE, MARJORIE: *A Portrait of Aristotle.* Chicago, U. of Chicago Press, 1963.

*Paperback Book

*JAEGER, WERNER: *Aristotle: Fundamentals of the History of His Development*. London, Oxford Paperbacks, 1962.

McKEON, RICHARD: *Introduction to Aristotle*. New York, Modern Library, 1947.

McKEON, RICHARD: *The Basic Works of Aristotle*. New York, Random House, 1941.

*RANDALL, J.: *Aristotle*. New York, Columbia U. Press, 1960.

*ROSS, DAVID: *Aristotle*. New York, Meridian Books, 1959.

*ROSS, DAVID: *Aristotle Selections*. New York, Charles Scribner's Sons, 1938.

*TAYLOR, A. E.: *Aristotle*. New York, Dover Publications, 1956.

*Paperback Book

INDEX